# THE LITTLE #METOO BOOK FOR MEN

"*The Little #MeToo Book for Men* is a profoundly empathetic guide for men who are navigating a culture that pressures them to bury their humanity. This book is nothing short of a blueprint for men's liberation."
**Caroline Heldman, Ph.D.**
**Executive Director,**
**The Representation Project**

"*The Little #MeToo Book for Men* is an excellent resource. It offers insight into our collective socialization and how we can break out of the Man Box to promote healthy manhood and help prevent all forms of violence and discrimination against all women and girls."
**Tony Porter, founder, A CALL TO MEN**

"Outstanding read and great contribution to understanding the current cultural impact on boys and healthy masculine development."
**Joe Ehrmann, Author, InSideOut Coaching**

"Mark Greene manages to write in a way that makes a very difficult topic easily accessible. His non-judgmental writing allows men to have a little distance, so they can think through these issues without shutting down. He places society and our culture squarely in the cross hairs and then offers men a path forward and out of the pain we inflict on others and ourselves when we blindly follow the cultural scripts we were born into. I will be recommending this book to my clients as well as friends and family."
**Jay Sefton, Therapist**

"A powerful and important set of lessons and reflections on 'the man box' and how it hurts and limits men, women, children, and all of us anywhere on the gender spectrum. Brief, clear, essential."
**Gene Combs, Co-Director, The Evanston Family Center**

**More videos, articles and resources at RemakingManhood.com**

This book is dedicated to my partner in life,
Dr. Saliha Bava.
Without our years of collaborative conversations,
my body of work simply wouldn't exist.

This book is also gratefully dedicated to
my father Arthur Wellington Greene, Jr.
"And one more for the pot."

# CONTENTS

"We must always take sides. Neutrality helps the oppressor, never the victim. Silence encourages the tormentor, never the tormented. Sometimes we must interfere."

- Elie Wiesel

## INTRODUCTION

*Before I begin, I'd like to acknowledge Riane Eisler's groundbreaking work on the domination system. Her work is central to my own exploration of our domination-based culture of masculinity.*

The Little #MeToo Book for Men is a critique of our dominant culture of masculinity in America, framed through the lens of a single challenging question. *Why is #MeToo such a source of alarm for so many men?* This book is the result of ten years of my writing and speaking about manhood as a senior editor for the Good Men Project. It is written from the perspective of a white man raised in the United States, but I am told these issues resonate globally, that men and women are dealing with versions of these issues everywhere.

•••

For millions of men, masculinity can seem like a foregone conclusion, mapped out for us by universally understood rules for being a "real man." These rules determine how we walk, how we talk, what we think and do, what we view as our responsibilities and most importantly, how we pursue or fail to pursue our deepest needs, wants and desires.

These rules of masculinity become so central to what we believe as to render the distinction between ourselves and our culture of masculinity invisible to us.

When millions of men live our lives subject to the rules of a culture we are not fully conscious of, it can be damaging for our families, our communities, our collective quality of life, and our longevity. As such, this book seeks to encourage a conversation about how boys and men arrive at what we believe.

If this conversation can reveal even the slightest glimmer of daylight between our dominant culture of masculinity and our own daily choices as men, my hope is we will find, in that space, a more vibrant and authentic connection to our agency, our power and our humanity.

Mark Greene
March 2021
New York City

# 1 /COLLISION

We cannot understand why #MeToo is so alarming for many men without also understanding our dominant culture of masculinity. The two are inescapably intertwined. We must look at how our culture of masculinity is constructed, what it creates in the world and how it impacts people's lives.

Cultures are not monolithic. Nor are they static. They are fluid and ever changing. Our dominant culture of masculinity coexists and overlaps with a multitude of other cultures, each rising and waning across generations. Cultures can be religious, corporate, political or social, based sometimes on rigid delineations of, and at other times the intermingling of, class, race, gender, creed and other categories of social identity.

What then, is culture? Culture is a collective agreement on how we should behave, integrated into how we construct our identities, and reconfirmed daily in our actions. Those with more power and resources often have more say in how we define culture. Those with less power often resist those definitions.

Our collective agreement about how men should behave has been shaped and reshaped over time. Whenever we decide to do so, we shift towards a new collective agreement, changing what we believe it means to be a man, sometimes by great leaps and bounds, sometimes by only the slightest of degrees. This process is ongoing, caught up in the push and pull of generations, gender, race, sexuality, religion, politics and the larger culture.

The more dominant a culture, the more those who have internalized it will fight in defense of it. The more archaic and inflexible a culture, the more it will be challenged as it increasingly fails to meet the needs of those who's lives it impacts. What has always been and what is coming next eventually come into direct conflict. Hence the term, culture war. The resulting collision can be chaotic, alarming and filled with challenges, creating great uncertainty daily or even hourly, disrupting our sense of who we are and how our world operates.

As women take up the banner of #MeToo by the millions, many men are feeling conflicted, alarmed, angry, and even disheartened. How is it that men are challenged by a movement which says, "Don't rape, sexually harass or abuse other human beings"? These are ideas we can all get behind, right? But it's not playing out that way.

The uncertainty and alarm this movement creates for

men can be profound, lurching up from within our culturally constructed identities, from within the process by which we experience and express who we are, and from within the powerful structures by which we are assigned our status.

Men have our own #MeToo stories, when we ourselves were sexually harassed, assaulted, or raped. These stories, which men have been shamed into hiding or denying, are just one more example of why this earthquake called #MeToo shakes the ground beneath all our feet. #MeToo challenges from multiple angles men's sense of control over, and confidence in, who we are. "Life used to be simple. Now it is complicated. Men and women used to know our place. Now we do not. I do not want to think about this."

#MeToo will go down in history as one of the most powerful cultural/political flash points in American history. While #MeToo calls out to our better angels, it also compels men to make a fundamental reassessment of everything we have suppressed, denied or taken for granted about our own masculine identities. Which makes talking about #MeToo the single conversation many men do NOT want to have.

The dangers of acknowledging, much less advocating for women within our social circles is well known to us. There are terrible and dark sides to the world of men, where alpha males display their strutting locker room dominance, daring any to challenge their open contempt for women, before blithely heading home to their wives and daughters to sit down for Sunday dinner.

In this way, generations of men have been bullied into averting our eyes from the ugly and abusive duality of our relationship with women. But it is precisely the dark disdain for women, threaded through our initiation into manhood, that has led us all to #MeToo.

## 2 /EPIDEMIC

In the early 1980's, Paul Kivel, Allan Creighton and others at the Oakland Men's Project developed "the Act Like a Man Box" in their work with adolescents in public schools around the San Francisco Bay Area. In 1992, Kivel documented their workshop process in his book *Men's Work: How to Stop the Violence That Tears Our Lives Apart*. As Kivel explains, it was here that they first framed their man box concept.

> "We invited boys and men to explore the cultural rules by which they had been socialized to conform to narrow definitions of masculinity, police each others' manhood and use their power and privileges to enforce gender-based exploitation, violence, and abuse against women, LGBTQ people, and other marginalized groups."

Following years of doing men's work in penitentiaries and other challenging spaces, Tony Porter, the founder of A CALL TO MEN, rephrased Kivel's term.

"Paul was on it, no question about that," Porter says. "He was on it. But the way he was saying it would not work for the men I was talking to. So, I took that term, 'act like a man box,' and I shortened it down to 'the man box.'"

Then, in 2010, Tony Porter's explosively popular TED Talk titled "A Call to Men" was seen by millions, driving the man box into our collective public consciousness.

Kivel's act like a man box refers to the *enforcement* of a narrowly defined set of traditional rules for being a man. These rules are enforced through shaming and bullying, as well as promises of rewards, the purpose of which is to force conformity to our domination-based culture of masculinity.

Because man box culture begins impacting boys at birth, by age three and four they are already engaging in a pecking order of bullying as proof of their manhood. Our sons are given no choice but to see bullying and domination as central mechanisms for forming and expressing male status and identity.

This culture of bullying has a deeply isolating effect on boys, shutting down their authentic expression, emotional acuity and suppressing their relational development. The isolating impact of man box culture is at the heart of men's epidemic levels of loneliness, addiction, depression, violence and suicide. Until we wake up and understand that our culturally induced disconnection in the world is quite literally killing us, it will continue to kill us every damn day.

Which is why this conversation about manhood has to happen. If we, as men, cannot do this for ourselves, caught up in our indecision about simple moral imperatives, angry and defensive, then we must summon the courage to have this conversation for those we love. We must find the strength to create a healthier masculinity of connection for our children and grandchildren, who deserve to grow up in a world free of the brutal inequality that we, by our collective indecision, are maintaining.

For men, to self-reflect about #MeToo is both life affirming and deeply challenging. To be able to question and reconsider who we are and what we believe, is a capacity that has never been valued in man box culture. Yet here we stand, confronted with a choice. We can avert our eyes from the hard truths of #MeToo or we can engage and, in the process, unpack years or even decades of man box conditioning, the price of which has been the loss of our authentic connection in the world.

Rethinking our role as men holds the very real promise of improving every single metric by which we measure quality of life, up to and including how long we will live.

But whether we like it or not, the days when #MeToo was somebody else's problem are long gone. No one is a bystander any more. Too many boys and men are being manipulated into attacking women, opposing progress and abusing each other. The denigration of women is directly linked to white supremacist recruitment. As the Southern Poverty Law Center states, "In many ways, white supremacy and male supremacy are one and the same."

It turns out that the war on women is also a war on

men. Our fathers, brothers and sons are literally dying from a lack of community and connection in the world.

It's well past time to pick a side. And what are the sides? The sides are simple: equity, yes or no. We are confronting a moment of truth based on a simple moral imperative: *that all human beings are created equal.*

## 3 /COLLAPSE

Ask men, regardless of where we are on the political spectrum, and we'll tell you. Something feels off. Something is not right. Daily we feel it, a surging dislocation, a weary dissatisfaction, and a restless sense of growing anxiety. It's the kind of discomfort you feel as you slowly realize the game you have been playing is rigged. All our lives we have been cheated, and we are coming to understand this in ever greater numbers.

From some quarters, men's voices are angry and reactive. They say that men are not allowed to be men; that women are taking over. Others feel deeply uncertain, wondering how to engage, even support movements like #MeToo without getting caught up in the binary crossfire of our culture wars.

The fight for women's equity is creating upheaval that is explosive in its implications for men's core sense of identity. #MeToo is a particularly timely earthquake, coming at a liminal moment in history when much of what once underpinned men's identities, both social and economic, is collapsing.

Go to any middle school or high school classroom in America. Ask the boys there to tell you the rules for being a man. They'll all tell you the same things. Always be tough. Always be successful. Always be confident. Always have the last word. Always be the leader. But one of the first rules of manhood these boys will tell you is that "real men" don't show their emotions.

The implications of this single prohibition run deep, informing nearly every aspect of men's, and by extension, women's lives. To this day, we coach our sons to present a facade of emotional toughness and our daughters to admire that facade in men. Even in infancy, little boys are expected to begin modeling stoicism, confidence, physical toughness, authority, and dominance. The strong and silent type remains a central American symbol of how to be a "real man."

These man box rules for being a "real man," are the reason why retrogressive nostalgia for a bygone 1950's era America is so compelling for some men. That earlier America, where large numbers of women were forced to accept their status as second-class citizens, provided the cultural container that made man box culture seemingly rewarding for men, and its catastrophic personal costs relatively invisible.

But now, after a century or more of women's

hard-fought battle towards equality, the remnant of our retrogressive 1950's era cultural container is collapsing. As it does, the brutal and isolating costs of man box culture become more evident to men, minus the countervailing benefits it once provided when women (and people of color, and LGBTQ people, and immigrants, and so many others) had no choice but to play along.

In this liminal cultural space between what was and what will be, men are experiencing deep uncertainty. Long reliant on the predictable command and control hierarchy of our culture of masculinity, we have never been taught to manage uncertainty, while women, who have historically been subject to the whims of men, have had to manage it all their lives.

Because men's man-box-constructed identities are based not on creating and maintaining authentic relationships and communities, but instead on a strict adherence to hierarchical roles, the loss of the cultural container that validates those roles feels like a terrifying loss of core identity.

## 4 /WHAT IS LOST

For generations, men have been conditioned to compete for status, forever struggling to rise to the top of a vast Darwinian pyramid framed by a simple but ruthless set of rules. But the men who compete to win in man box culture are collectively doomed to fail, because the game itself is rigged. We're wasting our lives chasing a fake rabbit around a track, all the while convinced there's meat to be had. There is no meat. We are the meat.

The slow realization that we can never win is the half-realized source of the male panic and rage surging through our culture. Like many men, I've wasted decades of my life trying to perform the man box model of masculinity, which by design leaves us struggling to prove our manhood in a culture that makes it impossible to ever completely do so.

Man box culture is deeply ingrained in us because it begins exerting its influence in the days after we are born. As little boys we begin suppressing our own naturally occurring capacities for emotional acuity and relational connection, thus setting us on a path for a lifetime of isolation. The damage is done before we are even old enough to understand what is happening.

The list of central relational capacities that man box culture suppresses includes empathy. The suppression of boys' and men's empathy is no accident. It is the suppression of empathy that makes a culture of ruthless competition, bullying and codified inequality possible. It is in the absence of empathy that men fail to see women's equality and many other social issues for what they are: simple and easily enacted moral imperatives.

It is remarkable that in spite of our man box culture, many men continue to fight for connection, community and equity in the world. But this happens in spite of everything man box culture does to us. Imagine a world where we encourage every boy's relational intelligence instead of suppressing it.

Imagine a world without the man box.

# 5 /THE MAN BOX

I have to give the man box its due. This particular trap we have collectively created? It is a truly nasty piece of work. Man box culture enforces a short, clear set of rules for being a "real man":

"Real men" don't show our emotions.

"Real men" are heterosexual, never homosexual, hyper-masculine, and sexually dominant.

"Real men" never ask for help.

"Real men" have control over women.

"Real men" are providers, never caregivers.

"Real men" are economically secure.

"Real men" are physically and emotionally tough.

"Real men" are sports focused.

These ways in which we are expected to prove our manhood are not about who we are, but about what we do: by what we earn, the points we score, who we bed, how we exercise, when we dominate, succeed, command, lead, fix and control.

In a world where our masculinity is based on what we do instead of who we are, men are reduced to the last paycheck we cashed, or the last woman we bedded, or the last ugly, wrenching pain we silently endured. This is the genius of man box culture. Our only choice is to keep going, pushing towards an end zone that recedes before us, ever a few more yards away. Ever a few more runs into the bruising defensive line, spread out before us, other men, their eyes fixed on some distant goalposts we can never see.

In her book, *When Boys Become Boys,* Dr. Judy Chu of Stanford University documents how our sons are taught to hide their early capacity for being emotionally perceptive, articulate, and responsive. Starting in preschool, our young sons learn to align their behaviors with "the emotionally disconnected stereotype our culture projects onto them."

Chu writes, "Boys are taught to hide vulnerable emotions like sadness, fear, and pain, which imply weakness and are stereotypically associated with femininity."

In her book, *Deep Secrets,* New York University professor and researcher Niobe Way shares the results from her years of research interviewing adolescent boys about their closest friendships. Way's research shows how our sons' joy in friendship and connection slowly atrophies over time, hammered away at by the message that needing or wanting close friendships is "childish, girly, or gay."

It is crucial that we acknowledge two points here:

- Boys are taught that their desire for close friendships is "girly or gay."
- This language reinforces daily that women and girls are less.

The cost is terribly high for all of us. In our isolating man box culture, boys entering late adolescence are shamed and bullied into seeing their close intimate male friendships as weak (feminine). Accordingly, they slowly disengage from these close friendships. It is at this time that suicide rates for boys rise, becoming four times the rate for girls (Way, 2011).

As we tell boys to "Man up" and "Don't be a sissy" what we're also communicating is "Don't be female, because female is less." Wrongly gendering the universal capacity for human connection as feminine and then conditioning boys to see feminine as less is how we block our sons from the trial and error process of growing their powerful relational capacities, leading to a lifetime of isolation.

At a time when boys should be expressing and constructing their identities in more diverse, grounded, and authentic ways, they are brutally conditioned to suppress authentic expression and instead cleave closely to the expression of male dominance as identity. And so, men brag about hook-up sex and ghosting women, seeking to bond via the uniformly degrading and contemptuous narratives of locker-room talk.

The result? Boys are bullied and shamed into being anti-women and anti-self, hiding those authentic aspect of themselves forbidden by the man box, even as they compete to parade their male privilege. The impact of women's progress toward equality on these men's core sense of identity cannot be underestimated. It is because women's equality is antithetical to how man box culture constructs male identity that some men are alarmed and angered by women's progress, engaged in a fierce battle to undo the advances women have made.

Meanwhile, because the need for close friendships is shamed in boys and men, we settle for friendships of proximity, surface-level relationships at our workplace, at the PTA or the gym. These friendships are interchangeable. If we change gyms, we drop that set of friendships and pick up the next ones. "What difference does it make? They're all the same. Right?."

Should men momentarily fail to conform to any of the rules of the man box, we are quickly policed to get back in line. What may begin for us as external policing eventually becomes our internal voice. "I need to make more money. I'm a pussy for feeling unsure of myself. I'm too slow, too fat, too weak."

The low-level anxiety this internal policing creates becomes baseline for us because in man box culture we can never get enough success, confidence or security. There will never be enough of anything. Maybe getting more money or sex will help. And back on the wheel we go.

For the record, man box culture is not traditional masculinity. The two are not equivalent. Man box culture refers to the *enforcement* of a narrow, cherry-picked, set of rules for masculinity. This is a crucial distinction. For some men, a place somewhere on the spectrum of tradition-based masculinities, is a good fit for them.

Man box culture rears its ugly head when its narrow rules of manhood are forced on all boys and men, seeking to stamp out our rich, diverse range of masculinities, traditional or otherwise.

For the courageous men who push back against man box culture, doing manhood differently can get them ostracized, dumped, shamed, fired, beaten or murdered. And even when we try to conform to the rules of man box culture, there are thousands of ways to falter, to fail, to miss a step.

Man box culture was never designed to let men succeed, to let us win. It was designed to keep men policing, and bullying, and ultimately, fearing each other.

## 6 /ANGRY VOICES

As men age in man box culture, we realize with growing anxiety that we can't keep proving our manhood forever. Maybe the paychecks aren't coming, or our knees are failing, or the one-liners aren't working, or whatever. Eventually, the system of manhood we bought into dumps us by the side of the road and barrels on, fueled by a new generation of younger, hungrier men; new dogs to chase the rabbit, more hamsters on the wheel.

Our winner-take-all man box culture eventually delivers on its promise. It has always told us what it is. *Maybe we weren't listening?* A few people at the top win, the rest get erased.

And it's only getting worse. A central component of 1950s America was a booming post-war economy and job security for men (not women), which underpinned for millions of working men the central man box role of being a provider. But the dog-eat-dog ethos of the man box ultimately led to an America where off-shoring jobs, short selling sub-prime mortgages, and creating predatory healthcare business models are just examples of someone doing the man box right. This means millions of men have been robbed of our primary role as providers within the very model of manhood that makes "providing" a central marker of our success. The result? Unemployment and economic hardship is driving alarming rates of suicide among older working-age men.

And so, as the curtain falls, aging American men are isolated and disconnected, left to express the only emotion we have ever been granted permission to express: anger. And true to our man box training, we direct our anger at anyone other than ourselves.

To admit we have been tricked would go against every rule of man box culture. It would require that we acknowledge our own agency in all of this. It would require we admit that our steadfast reliance on dominance and certainty, our obsession with America's cult of bootstrap individualism, has ultimately failed us. It would require a reassessment of our priorities, our beliefs and our view of others. Most of all, it would require self-reflection, a capacity we were never taught by a culture of masculinity that does not care who we are as individuals. And when our anger ultimately turns back on ourselves, men commit suicide in ever growing numbers because we don't have a robust community of male friendships we can turn to in a crisis.

How have men been cheated? We look up one day,

and we discover we have been robbed of the authentic relationships and robust community that for hundreds of thousands of years, literally from the dawn of humankind, have given human beings their purpose and meaning. Instead, we sit in our gated communities before our big screen TVs and we are alone, distrustful of others, and fearful of anyone different, anyone who is not us. We have been bullied by the man box into swapping the fundamental joy of human connection for an empty, isolating, alpha male pecking order. We become like dogs chained up alone in the back of the yard, howling and crazy.

The constant drumbeat of male rage that floods our media and surges up in our national politics is rooted in the collective self-alienation and social isolation that defines our man box culture of masculinity. The result for men is epidemic levels of divorce, depression, addiction, suicide, violence, and mass shootings.

Men got cheated. Yes, we did. *And everyone else is paying the price.*

# 7 /BILLY THE BULLY

Woke Daddy blogger Ludo Gabriele published a blog post titled, "The Sordid (Yet Insightful) Tale of a Panic Attack." It's a courageous and vulnerable glimpse into one man's collapse into terror. It implores us to look more closely at how the man box operates for men in our culture. Even woke men. Even me.

The internalized voice of the cop-in-our-head that Ludo describes (he calls him Billy the Bully) generates the low-level anxiety that many men feel daily as we look over our shoulder, watching to see if we're being judged, about to be called out. "What are you, a sissy? What are you, a momma's boy?," and so on.

When the constant stress and fear of being policed within the man box gets to be too much, when booze or drugs or sex won't calm the anxiety any more, the cop-in-our-head offers us a "get out of jail free card," an instant pass to the front of the line. We can simply vent our anxiety, by shaming and policing someone else. Bully a skinny kid.

Beat up a gay man. Ghost a woman. Acts of dominance, both large and small required of us to confirm our standing in man box culture are its most insidious component. In one simple act, we both reinforce man box culture and confirm in our own minds that we deserve to take abuse if we fail to conform adequately.

Sooner or later, this ugly loop of policing gets located entirely within ourselves. Other men don't even have to call us out anymore. The cop-in-our-head, Billy the Bully, reminds us daily that we can fail at any moment, that we are being watched. To prove to Billy we are with the program, we batter the more connecting, joyful human parts of ourselves into submission. "See, Billy? I showed him."

In The Will To Change, bell hooks writes,

> "The first act of violence that patriarchy demands of males is not violence toward women. Instead patriarchy demands of all males that they engage in acts of psychic self-mutilation, that they kill off the emotional parts of themselves. If an individual is not successful in emotionally crippling himself, he can count on patriarchal men to enact rituals of power that will assault his self-esteem."

And because man box culture trains us to suppress our need for human connection and authentic male friendships, we have lost the central mechanism by which we can ask for support. Our authentic, joyful connection in the world is beaten out of us, leaving us alone in the dark with Billy the Bully.

*And Billy wants us dead.*

# 8 /EPIDEMIC OF ISOLATION

A 2010 AARP study estimates that one in three Americans aged 45 and older (that's 42 million people) are chronically lonely, up from one in five Americans ten years before. Cigna released a 2018 study, which shows that "Nearly half of Americans report sometimes or always feeling alone." The Cigna study goes on to say, "Generation Z (adults ages 18–22) is the loneliest generation and claims to be in worse health than older generations."

Man box culture is a central contributor to our epidemic of loneliness, and loneliness is a killer. Chronic loneliness is as high a risk factor for mortality as smoking, increasing the likelihood of cancer, diabetes, heart disease, Alzheimer's disease, obesity, depression, and a raft of other illnesses. Cancer metastasizes faster in lonely people. For millions of men, loneliness is killing us before our time.

Jay Sefton, a licensed mental health counselor, recently made the following observation regarding opiate addiction on the website, Medium:

"The culture of male suppression is often a key underlying issue for men struggling with addiction. I see it frequently in my practice and it's true in my own battle with alcoholism. The pressure to adhere to cultural roles and scripts for males in our society is so pervasive that we generally don't notice it running in the background.

It's like the quiet that descends during a power outage — we're not aware of how loud ambient electricity is until it is gone. Perhaps someone is treated for an injury and didn't realize the psychological pain that was present until the pain medication relieved it. Once we finally get relief, we never want the pain back again. Unfortunately, drugs and alcohol always fail in the long run to deliver on the promise of removing pain caused by the toxic elements of our culture. We must instead rely on radical compassion and love to offer real healing."

# 9 /#METOO

Lisa Hickey, the publisher and CEO of the Good Men Project has a simple point to make about #MeToo.

The #MeToo campaign was originally created in 2007 by activist Tarana Burke in response to stories of sexual assault she was hearing from girls and women. #MeToo had a huge upsurge in prominence on October 15, 2017, when the actress Alyssa Milano tweeted, "If you have been sexually harassed or assaulted, write 'me too' in response to this tweet."

The resulting outpouring of #MeToo stories exploded across social media, eventually numbering in the millions. For Hickey, the singular intention of Milano's tweet was fulfilled — demonstrating the scale of the problem.

#MeToo is about witnessing and solidarity among victims of sexual harassment, abuse, assault or rape. Any person who takes issue with #MeToo is taking issue, first and foremost, with people saying "Yes, this happened to me, too."

While men are often victims of sexual assault and rape, for the purposes of this discussion we will be talking about how our dominant culture of masculinity leaves women vulnerable to sexual assault. And how we, as men, can change this.

In the National Intimate Partner and Sexual Violence Survey, the U.S. Centers for Disease Control and Prevention reports that "Approximately 1 in 5 (21.3% or an estimated 25.5 million) women in the U.S. reported completed or attempted rape at some point in their lifetime." Given that many women don't report sexual assault, the actual number is much higher.

Yet, there are some men who will insist that these numbers are inflated. Some among us will debate how many millions of rapes are actually taking place. Is it actually fifteen million? Ten million? What kind of culture of masculinity is capable of hosting a debate on rape framed in terms of how many millions are actually being raped, instead of how to stop it?

Ours is.

Imagine ten women you know personally. Statistically, two of them are likely to be rape survivors. Which two? We don't know, do we? Now imagine your child's or any child's classroom. Picture any ten of those little girls. Which two of them will be rape survivors? Are we there, yet? Are we feeling a little sick?

Because this is the place men need to get to on the question of #MeToo.

If men want to really and truly help, the central challenge we must collectively address is how we are trained from an early age to normalize a whole range of "lesser" acts of sexual harassment and abuse against girls and women. These abusive acts include cat calling, rape jokes and locker room talk, among many others.

In constantly asserting their right to perpetrate abusive acts against girls and women, some men have bullied the rest of us into silently accepting, for example, that all women will have to deal with cat calling on the street. And this is just one example of the normalization of abuse. Our dominance-based culture of masculinity actively normalizes abusive behavior in all facets of women's personal and professional lives.

When a man at the office says to a group of men around him, "She has a real nice ass," it's important to understand this kind of public statement for what it is, for the function it serves in reinforcing dominance-based masculine culture.

Of course, good guys like us are rolling our eyes or walking away thinking, "Some guys are jerks and will say stuff about women, but what the hell, I'm not going to get into it." And in our silence, we allow to remain in place the ongoing assertion that the denigration of women is just part of manhood. "Some men are just that way."

A while back, a guy posted this on my Facebook feed:

"Locker-room talk is just that. It is all talk and does not make you a predator." The idea being, that locker-room talk is harmless. It's just what men do.

Engaging in locker-room talk doesn't make us predators, but it most certainly perpetuates a culture in which predators can hide. The term "locker-room talk" is literally designed to grant permission, even encourage men to speak in this way, as if locker rooms exist in some magical man-only world. Every male social space that exists has an impact on women's lives because our words as men go with us, change us, inform what we do next.

Our denigration of women, or our choice to remain silent when others do so, takes place in a world populated by the women and girls who must coexist with us, along with the words, ideas, and predators we grant refuge to.

*11th Principle: Consent!'s gender neutral Rape Culture Pyramid is a powerful representation of these issues and more. Go have a look at 11thPrincipleConsent.org.*

## 10 /DON'T MESS WITH JOE

Men's overwhelming tendency to remain silent in the face of the daily denigration of women, supports the continuing normalization of sexual harassment and violence against girls and women. When men are challenged with this argument, we often push back. "I'm not a rapist, my friends aren't rapists. You're calling us all rapists."

So, let's be clear. No one is collectively calling all men rapists. What we're saying is millions of men are choosing to remain silent about the abusive behavior we often witness, and this allows for a culture which puts women in danger. What's more, we aren't even fully conscious of why we chose to remain silent.

*Facts: One in five women in the United States report they are survivors of attempted or completed rape. Millions more don't report it when they are sexually assaulted.*

Man box culture contributes to the normalization of sexual assault when it encourages men to denigrate women as part of our performance of masculinity. And even though millions of us don't agree with this behavior, we are conditioned to avoid conflict with other men when they do this. This is because the men who openly degrade women are primed to attack us as well. They are the alpha bullies of man box culture, and the first rule of avoiding them is to avoid any defense of women. In this way, men have been conditioned over a lifetime to avoid the #MeToo conversation like the plague.

When Joe, the manager at the office, says, "She's got a nice ass" to a group of men at the water cooler, we immediately peg Joe as a certain kind of man. And we are confronted with a choice. To call him out or not. "Joe, don't say that stuff," is all it would take, but Joe's public denigration of women tells us who his next target would be. Because Joe isn't only degrading women at the office, he's also trolling the men around him, testing for who might disagree. He is declaring his politics and his power.

If any among us challenges Joe, he will instantly redirect his contempt from women to us. "Oh, I see how it is. You want to have sex with her? What, are you some kind of feminist?"

Catalyst, a global non profit dedicated to helping build workplaces that work for women, states that "many men want to intervene and reduce sexism—yet sometimes do not." Catalyst's groundbreaking 2021 study found that "men at work often experience 'masculine anxiety'—distress over not living up to society's rigid masculine standards. The study also revealed that men with high masculine anxiety are likely to say they would do nothing in the face of workplace sexism. Masculine anxiety, which is exacerbated by a combative culture at work, is widespread. Nearly all men (99%) indicated that their workplace has some level of combative culture."

The metaphor I use for what is created by combative work cultures is "suppressing fire," designed to suppress the willingness of the men around him to call out Joe's sexist behavior. Meanwhile, Joe is openly and vocally asserting women's second-class status, because without that single central premise stringently enforced, his man-box-constructed identity collapses. In the moment that women gain full equity, Joe loses them as symbols of his superior status and he loses them as the central issue by which he trolls and polices men around him.

We know that challenging Joe can affect our social standing in the office, the projects we are assigned, our ongoing stress levels and so on, because we know that once Joe marks us as a target, we will stay a target. Accordingly, standing up for one woman can put the financial security of our family at risk. And because our man box culture suppresses any larger conversations, we don't know what the other men in the circle are thinking. Most likely, "For god's sake, don't make waves." And Joe the Bully wins. Again.

Boys and men are conditioned over the course of their lifetimes by the Joes of the world. In order not to run afoul of Joe, we learn to base our performance of manhood on the anti-feminine, anti-connection model of man box culture, leaving us siloed and isolated and thus, more easily managed in a command and control structure.

But what's also important to understand is that after years of man box conditioning, we might even grudgingly admire Joe. This is because what Joe is doing feels powerful to us. It seems like masculine strength. We respect the force of this kind of display even as we might deplore the intent. It takes great strength of will for boys and men to set aside our conditioning and directly challenge Joe. It's much easier to dismiss the Joes of the world and walk away. "Joe is a jerk. Forget about Joe."

And herein lies the central problem. While Joe's message about women is public, our refusal to accept it is private. We have no impact. We have no voice, the result of years of suppressing fire we have undergone at the hands of boys and men like Joe.

We have been systematically trained all our lives into silence by men who constantly signal their readiness to escalate any comment in support of women to an attack on our manhood. While this training begins in our earliest years with the denigration of women, ultimately, this suppressing fire extends across a much wider range of political and social issues.

Bias begins with the denigration of women because unlike almost any other bias, anti-feminine bias can be taught globally to boys regardless of class, race, religion, age or nationality. Anti-feminine conditioning then becomes a powerful and universal gateway to inculcating other forms of bias.

When we teach our sons "You are better then girls," instead of teaching them, "Don't put others down to make yourself feel better," we prime their vulnerability to all forms of bigotry.

"You are better than gays. you are better than Blacks. You are better than Jews. You are better than immigrants. You are better than the poor," and so on.

This is why our silence on the issue of the denigration of women is so damaging, leaving those who are the most aggressive and the loudest to define our culture of masculinity as a culture of inequality. As men, we must stop saying to ourselves, "I'm one of the good guys. I'm protecting and providing for the women in my family. I will focus on keeping them safe. On empowering them."

It's a nice idea, but it simply won't work. Sooner or later, they will have to go out on their own and the Joes of the world will be waiting for them. Because man box culture is threaded through with contempt for the feminine as a primary method for suppressing boy's emotional and relational development, the end result is a culture of sexual violence against women.

We can not keep the women in our family or our circle of friends safe by remaining silent. Through our inaction, we sustain the foundation of the pyramid of sexual abuse insuring a world in which millions of women will be raped.

*In our silence we are culpable.*

## 11 /FALSE ACCUSATIONS

Some men; alarmed and angered by the #MeToo movement are actively working to undermine it. The most prominent strategy they use is to raise the specter of false rape allegations.

These "Joe the Bullies" of the world are working overtime to stoke our doubts by loudly questioning women's stories of assault and rape. "Did she remember correctly? Is she giving all the details? Is she confused? Was she drinking? What was she wearing? Why was she there alone? Why didn't she report it sooner? Who can confirm her story?" And the most horrendous of all, "We believe she was assaulted, we just don't think she's remembering correctly who it was."

I have spoken on our culture of masculinity to rooms full of thoughtful, considerate people, willing to talk about the most challenging issues we face, yet many still raise their hands and ask, "What about false sexual assault allegations?"

The question for me is, how is it that men are able to doubt allegations of sexual abuse after growing up in our man box culture? We know the levels of bullying and violence it's capable of only too well. This questioning of women's recollections, motivations and honesty could only take place in a world where the majority of men fear to question or challenge those who defend abusers. Instead, we look for excuses to avoid owning our own silence. We latch on to the slightest bit of doubt generated by the false-accusations-of-rape argument and give ourselves permission to look away.

There are no legitimate statistics supporting the myth of widespread false rape accusations, but here are statistics on rape as reported by RAINN (Rape, Abuse & Incest National Network). Out of every thousand instances of rape, thirteen cases get referred to a prosecutor, and only seven cases will lead to a felony conviction. Conclusion, most rapes are not reported to law enforcement at all.

Being concerned about the very unlikely possibility of false rape allegations instead of our epidemic of rape and assault is immoral. Believe survivors, boy and girls, men and women, alike. The supposed threat of false rape accusations is a smokescreen designed to sow enough doubt that men take the easy out and remain silent. That's all abusers ask of us, to remain silent.

And there is that word again. Silence. Every aspect of man box culture ultimately triangulates on a single male capacity, our voices, replacing our authentic expression with bullying scripts against other men and women. Raising the very real threat that if we speak up in defense of common human decency we will be shamed and attacked.

While some men complain that women won't let "men be men," what is astounding is how meekly these same men accept the daily and even hourly policing of our masculinity by other men, seemingly without complaint. "Oh, sorry," we say. We tuck our tails when the alpha male bullies order us about and we accept domination by men who are stripping from us our most basic of human rights, the right to live our lives as distinct and authentic human beings.

Ultimately, it isn't the bullies who control American masculinity. It is the silence of the much more sizable majority of men, who carry enough trauma that we avoid standing up for ourselves and the women in our lives. We are collectively silenced, confused and suppressed, traumatized into sacrificing ourselves, our families and our communities on the altar of man box culture.

And the powerful people at the top of man box culture are laughing at us.

# 12 /SUPPRESSING FIRE

Let's do a little thought experiment.

Women earn about eighty cents for every dollar earned by men, for equal work. The gap is often larger among higher-paying jobs.

How many men have a female life partner who is a working woman? Yet, collectively, men accept a 20% shortfall in our partners' income level, simply because, you know, ...women.

That's a new car. That's a vacation. That's a dishwasher. Why isn't every man with a working female spouse or life partner out in the streets demanding that equal pay become the law of the land? Forget fairness for women. Forget morality or ethics. These are our families' bank balances we're talking about.

Over a decade or two, this 20% gap can be the difference between borrowing for or paying cash for a child's college education. It can be a retirement fund. It can be a rental property or health insurance. Yet we continue to live in a nation in which men accept lower pay for our own family members, wives, sisters, and mothers, which is clearly yet another example of male silence playing out. How do we know this? Because if all the men who have a working female spouse got behind pay equity tomorrow, it would be the law of the land the day after.

Instead, we collectively shrug.

"Oh, yeah, that's a thing. Women get paid less. But what are you going to do?" isn't going to cut it. And as much as it should be framed as an issue of simple fairness, that's not the point I am making here, either.

That millions of men are voluntarily giving up such a sizable sum of money must mean we're exchanging it for something *we value more.*

Are we truly exchanging our child's college fund for the illusion of status over women? Can we really be that easily manipulated? Or have decades of suppressing fire from Joe the Bully left us unwilling to challenge his dominant narrative that women are less. And because men in man box culture don't talk about this stuff (Sports only, boys...), do we then assume general agreement with Joe the Bully even though collectively, men might actually support having more money in their families' bank accounts?

It's no accident that many voices in media and politics model the angry bullying voice of man box culture, suppressing men's willingness to challenge demonstrably terrible policies for fear that the men in our networks will "kick us out of the club" or worse, that we will be shamed and abused all over again. Man box culture has bullied us into silence. As a result, any potential collective support for more progressive policies, even in our own immediate social circles, remains hidden from us.

The question is often posed, why do Americans so consistently vote against our own self-interest? Equal pay legislation is one example of this, bogged down as it has been for years in the U.S. Congress. In a pattern that plays out over and over across a wide range of issues, men are conditioned to act against our own communities, our families and ourselves. And for what do we give up so much?

This is the power of man box culture, that it can convince men to live shorter, more isolated, more impoverished lives in exchange for *the illusion of status over women.*

# 13 /MAPPING OUR SILENCE

Author and researcher Niobe Way has this to say about the first rule of the man box. "The simple message that to be a man you have to be emotionless; ... emotionless in the sense of invulnerable, is traumatic. And that leads to essentially everything else."

Our dominant culture of manhood is generations old, reaching far back in its scope and scale. It has been internalized by men and women alike, asserting itself almost universally from the earliest moments of our childhood.

In her book, When Boys Become Boys, Judy Chu writes about her time embedded in a pre-K classroom. Her research there lasted two years, following a group of children through to the end of their kindergarten year.

She tells the story of a four-year-old boy who revealed to her that, "All of the girls in the class are my friends, but I act as though they aren't ... because if Mike, the leader of the boys' club, finds out ... that I like the girls, he'll fire me from his club ... That would be a real bummer 'cause then I won't be in a club."

The challenging part of this four-year-old boy's story isn't just that he can't have girls as his friends. That's problematic enough, eliminating crucial years of learning how to relate and form friendships across gender in authentic and respectful ways. The central issue here is that at age four, this little boy is already taking parts of his more authentic relational self and silencing them out of fear of being kicked out of the boys' club. He is tracking and accommodating an alpha boy in a hierarchical structure that he is already accustomed to operating in.

And who is the leader of this boys' club? Even into adulthood, we always know who he is. Man box culture elevates him from an early age, winking at his transgressions and, when he goes too far, noting with a shrug that, "Boys will be boys." We grant him the heady and narcotic experience of controlling others in the name of being a leader. But we don't teach him what responsible, inclusive leadership is. And so, he very likely ends up becoming Joe the Bully, attacking and harassing any who challenge his position of dominance.

Meanwhile, the boys under his sway suppress their capacity to collaborate, co-create, innovate, empathize and bridge across differences with the children around them. His message to not talk to the girls is part of the first wave of silencing for very young boys, stripping them of the years of trial and error exploration of expression that is key to learning to relate and create relationships.

In this way, the gulf of difference, predicated by our

cartoonish gender binaries, is introduced and fostered. Boys' emotional acuity and joyous social natures are falsely gendered as feminine, shamed and suppressed. Girls are herded toward the garish gender stereotypes of the Disney princess, ironically awaiting a prince who, when he finally arrives, will likely have contempt for them. Non binary kids are devalued entirely.

Over the course of their lives, our sons' and daughters' natural capacities for connection fail to be developed via the relational back and forth by which humans develop nuance. Simplistic, limiting rules for performing gender are hammered home, enforcing a gender binary which, above all else, is about silencing our children's natural capacities to connect and relate. Then we declare the resulting dysfunction biological. We say that this is just how boys and girls are hardwired.

Meanwhile, man box culture's constant reliance on the denigration women and gays as the primary means for boys and men to confirm our masculinity means we have all been party to abusive comments or actions at some point in our lives. This leads to a powerful and silencing "integrity bind" for men. Meaning that those of us who do choose to speak up against the relentless abuses of man culture must do so with the understanding we are hypocrites on some level, breaking with our own histories in that moment. The likely response from the abusers we may decide to confront? "Oh, NOW you decide to speak up after doing the same stuff for years? You have no integrity, so shut up."

And, in fact, this is the exact response we see whenever individuals or organizations stand up for the first time against abuse toward women. It is one of the standard strategies by which man box culture seeks to protect itself, derailing the focus to a false notion of integrity when the conversation should be about the moral absolute of ending abuse.

And so, for millions of men, silence becomes more and more central to our performance of masculinity. Silence becomes the strategy by which we seek to protect our hard-won professional and social gains. But it's a strategy that will fail. Our society may have once been a place where men could avoid risking their status by simply staying quiet, but as our 1950s culture of inequality falters, the bullies and the alphas are asserting themselves. Threats of violence and abuse, even at the highest levels of government, have become commonplace. The assault on more civil discourse is growing. White and male supremacy is on the rise. Our cultural tipping point on masculinity can go either way, toward a culture of equity for all, or dramatically away from it.

Our families and our communities require not silence and survival from us, but our shared risk and leadership. If men, buffered as we are by our relative safety, remain silent at this crucial point, seeking to avoid conflict with the bullies and demagogues who are rising in this liminal space, something far uglier will take hold. Something that amplifies dominance-based masculine extremism so dramatically that our families, our security and everything else we hold dear will be at risk.

# 14 /COURAGE

I'm uncomfortable writing this, telling other men to step up. My culture has taught me not to do this, not to have this conversation. If you're a man, you may be uncomfortable reading it. But I can only offer you this. My condemnation of our culture of masculinity is NOT a condemnation of men. I do however, hold us responsible for our byllying dominance-based culture of masculinity if we fail to create something better.

Collectively, men still have a simple but important lesson to learn. Some of us learn this lesson at great cost, after a crisis of our own making, the loss of our careers or the collapse of our marriages. It's a lesson reflected in the voices of broken men at AA meetings. It's visible there in the shining eyes of fathers cradling their newborn children. It's a lesson reflected in the ancient philosophies and religions of the world.

The lesson is this. Despite what we have been taught, our power as men does not lie in how well we are able to dominate and control those around us. Dominance-based masculinity is, in fact, a recipe for early stress-related diseases, unhappiness, and violence. It is a direct threat to our families, our society and our world. Moreover, it is deeply and fundamentally isolating. And isolation is death.

Dominance-based man box culture conditions men to be change averse in a world that is fueled by ongoing change. It is a static wall of inertia, slowing the pace of our collective evolution and growth. The world will continue to evolve and grow. The only question is, how much human suffering, our own and others, will men create before we evolve, too? We can continue to allow man box culture to dominate us, or we can start fighting for our basic human freedoms. We can start pushing back, making space for a much more diverse range of masculinities, creating more options for how men can live their lives.

Millions of men are already doing this work, expanding boundaries and creating more fluid expressions of gender, especially among millennials. Millions of fathers are taking on the role of full-time parents and primary caregivers. Homophobia, long used to enforce the man box, is in decline among younger men.

As men, we can choose to engage our relational capacities for growing connection and community. When we marshal our courage and step into those socially dynamic spaces, stepping past false notions like the integrity bind, past the anxious false security of our own silence, we discover a world that is less predictable and more generative. In the process, we can learn from others how to sit with our uncertainty, embracing it as the natural byproduct of new ideas and processes being born.

The courageous choice for men is to lean into our uncertainty, against the weaker aspects of our natures that seek predictability and control over evolution and growth. In exploring and engaging uncertainty, we discover the heady awakening of our personal sense of adventure.

Know this: pushing back against man box culture will NOT get you kicked out of the club. There is no club. Man box culture is, by definition, isolation. Standing up against man box culture, at the cost of some of our surface level relationships, will open the door to more diverse, creative and authentic relationships, any one of which is invaluable by comparison.

It's well past time to marshal our courage and choose connection. It's time to create something better.

# 15 /THE ART OF RELATIONSHIPS

This chapter was written in cooperation with couple and family therapist, Dr. Saliha Bava. It is designed to share some relational practices that can be helpful in creating more supportive and generative conversations regardless of the subject. These capacities can be especially helpful in the context of #MeToo.

When we, as men, seek to engage and better understand women's lives and the #MeToo movement, we can choose first and foremost, to be mindful of context. Who are we seeking to connect with and what are the issues that underpin our relationship with those individuals? Remember, these are not conversations women are obligated to have with us. Go lightly. Be mindful. For those of us who are survivors, we know how challenging it can be to tell our own stories. If the offer to talk about our experiences makes us feel obligated to comply or worse, debated with or lectured to, then the trauma of our pasts is compounded.

We all have a wide range of relationships in our lives,

from deeply personal to more casual. These relationships can be with members of our families, with co-workers, with people in our neighborhoods, with others at our school or our local market. Understanding when and where it is appropriate to engage in a conversation about #MeToo is an important gateway to deciding to do so. Giving thought to the ways in which our approach to these conversations can be harmful or helpful is crucial.

For many men, the degree of sexual harassment and abuse the women may be facing, even daily, can be somewhat invisible to us. The women we know may have chosen long ago to keep their stories to themselves. For those who are close to us, we can perhaps begin with a simple question. Being mindful that we ask at the right time and in the right context, we can ask if they want to share their thoughts on how it is to be a woman. It seems a simple question, but it can open the door to many stories.

For men, inviting women to have this conversation can be challenging, both for others and for us. First and foremost, we must judge correctly whether or not there is a conversation to be had. For example, this is not necessarily a question to automatically ask of past romantic partners.

Additionally, some women report being hit with a barrage of questions that can easily be answered with a little research online. Women report men asking questions that seem to be searching for the "all clear." As challenging a time as this is, we need to keep a central message in mind. Women are asking men to do better. If our actions make room for others (men and women) to feel respected and safe, we have already made a huge contribution to the movement.

That said, the conversation about #MeToo and women's lives is one we can offer to have with women in our families, or women with whom we have close personal or professional relationships. There needs to be a degree of trust already in place for this conversation to happen, but it can be an opportunity to practice and grow powerful relational capacities.

## 1) LISTENING WITH CURIOSITY

Any conversation is an opportunity to listen, but a conversation about #MeToo allows someone close to you to speak into a space that may be entirely new for you both. As men, we might respond by attempting to fix or explain, as this is the role-based version of manhood we have been trained to perform. If we can instead seek to listen with curiosity as our friends, family members, or partners share their thoughts we can experience how powerful listening can be. It's a process by which we focus on relationships instead of our role.

Like most aspects of communication, listening can be less than helpful if reduced to a process by which we are simply waiting our turn to speak or preparing to engage in a debate. When we learn to listen with curiosity, a new process can take place. We can enter the conversation with the expectation of hearing something new and powerful. We can be curious, listening for things we do not expect, instead of focusing on the parts of a conversation that might reinforce our expectations. We can listen with the understanding that we're not here to fix or solve, but instead to allow others to simply speak out loud what they are feeling, which sometimes is all they need from us.

Not every woman has a story about surviving abuse. But when we do encounter stories of abuse or even rape that others sometimes share, it can be deeply challenging. In response, we might seek to express our anger at an abuser, look for solutions to the feelings being expressed, suggest actions to be taken, or in some other way try to fix the situation.

For many of us, this urge to fix things is actually born out of our own emotional discomfort. As men, we may not have had much practice sitting with the challenging emotions of others, of being there for people who are feeling grief or anger. We simply have had no practice doing this kind of work. So, in our discomfort at witnessing others pain or sadness, we end up trying to fix the problem, thinking in these moments, "There I fixed it for you, so don't show me those emotions anymore."

When men are in "fix the problem" mode, here are some of the kind of things we might be inclined to think or even say:

"I'm sorry it's this way, but this happens to a lot of people. You're not alone."

"Are you sure he or she meant it that way?"

"If you toughen up a little, these things won't bother

you so much."

"That happened a long time ago."

"For your own good, you need to move past this."

"You have had good relationships since then, right?"

Instead, we can try these kinds of responses:

"I'm sorry for what you went through."

"I hear what you are saying."

"How would you like for me to be listening right now?"

"How does it feel to be telling this story?"

"Would you like to pause and start again in a little while?"

What is central here is to avoid becoming emotional, expressing personal anger, seeking to define ourselves as different, or telling stories of how we might have been abused. There will be time later to share our stories. Think of hearing the stories of others as a sacred space. It is in this mindset that our most helpful responses will come to us.

## 2) ASKING QUESTIONS

Which brings us to the powerful relational capacity of asking questions. Often men and women pose questions in an effort to drive a conversation toward a solution. If questions are designed to point to solutions or challenge the assumptions of the person who is telling their story, it will not be a helpful process. When we instead ask questions that indicate our calm interest, that help the storyteller clarify what they are saying or feeling, it can have a calming and trust-building effect on both parties. When we take some time to just be a witness, we create a relational space in which our friend or partner can share what they need to share. Asking, "How would you like me to listen?" and, "Do you want to continue?" signals clearly that we are ready to create a calm and supportive space for them to share their story.

### 3) HOLDING UNCERTAINTY

When we engage in conversation with others, especially about challenging issues or subjects, we can often feel intense uncertainty. "Where is this conversation going to go?" For men, long trained to present confidence and leadership, we may feel compelled to seem knowledgeable and confident, even when we are actually feeling alarmed.

In order to be a calm engaged witness to the stories of others, we can work to grow our capacity to sit with the uncertainty that can arise. Over time, we can grow this capacity, but it can be challenging initially.

We can learn to manage our uncertainty, and the anxiety it can produce, in several ways:

Physically: We can take a moment to breathe deeply and calm our physical response.

Emotionally: We can check in with ourselves, reminding ourselves not to collapse into our emotions but instead focus on doing the important work of creating a calm space for our friend or partner to share their story.

Re-framing the experience: We can change our

relationship to uncertainty, seeing it instead as a sign that something new and powerful is emerging. Uncertainty can be a highly generative, creative space, once we give up the need to control what is coming next.

### 4) HOLDING IDEAS LIGHTLY

One powerful way to resist collapsing into the emotions that arise in the back and forth of difficult conversations, is to hold our ideas more lightly. When we do this, we are less inclined to filter for others' points of view that might seem to be in opposition to our own, and instead listen in a more holistic way, ensuring we can better hear all that is being communicated.

It is often our fears and concerns, born out of closely held beliefs, that block us from hearing all that others are saying. When we hold our ideas more lightly, we reduce our reactivity. This is not about giving up our beliefs. It is about not letting them limit the ways we can listen and connect in the world. It's about learning to co-design and collaborate across difference with others in our lives.

Relational practices like these center our personal and professional relationships as the primary source of our health and well being. In the daily back and forth of relating, we create and redesign who we are in partnership with those around us. It is in the mindful back and forth of relationships that we grow our sense of community, connection and joy.

*"When we seek for connection, we restore the world to wholeness."*
    *- Margaret J. Wheatley*

# 16 /MEN'S POWER

Men are in crisis. We are collectively traumatized and often deeply isolated. Our collective solution going forward is to create connection. Human beings rise or fall together. All of us.

For men, learning to relate, connect, and collaborate holds the key to breaking out of our man box culture. The movement for more wide ranging, diverse, and authentic masculinities holds the promise of reawakening for men nothing less than the art of being in relationship.

In order to undo the isolating impact of man box culture in our lives, men must take everything we have been taught about gender and flip it on its head. We must call up every relational capacity we were taught to deny, every capacity degraded and wrongly gendered as feminine, including empathy, play, compassion, collaboration, connection, and that greatest of human capacities, bridging across difference.

We can choose to come in from the cold, learning daily

to negotiate, explore, and play in the context of a world that remains trauma-inducing and trauma-informed. We can do the work of connection and self-reflection, knowing all the while that the trauma we seek to address in ourselves and others may not be fully resolved in our lifetimes.

We can gain powerful new capacities. We can learn to sit with the anxiety we feel, created by not knowing what is emerging while the human heart does its mysterious work. We can learn to sit with issues that will not be easily resolved and in doing so, perhaps, some day, resolve them.

Human beings heal in the moment by moment back and forth of relating and connecting. We don't heal in isolation. We heal in relationship. When we learn to connect in the sharing of our stories, something remarkable happens. We're not alone any more. We become family. We become community, and any of us — regardless of our histories, our challenges, or our past sins — can begin this work. We can make the world a safer and more joyful place. We can leave the anxiety behind. We can be free.

The first step is simple. We need only admit that we want authentic connection with others. What follows is the miracle of being human. Even if we have been bullied and trained out of forming relationships over the course of a lifetime, the capacity to fully connect remains, just beyond the door, waiting for us to let it back in. And there are others waiting to help us open that door.

Good, decent, empowered men are working to help

others rediscover their gifts for connection, based on the following simple truths. Men do not want to be angry. Men do not want to be alone. Men are not naturally inclined toward the toxic confines of the man box. If we were, it wouldn't be killing us.

Groups like the Mankind Project, Humen, Evryman and others are tearing down the walls of isolation that trap men in cycles of anger and reactivity. If you are a man who is struggling, who is tired of being alone, reach out to these men, or to other men's groups. When you enter a room full of men who are not judging you, not skeptical of you, not looking to undercut or dominate or reject you, the difference is like being able to breathe again. It's that powerful.

If you are a man, reading this book, consider this your personal invitation. In whatever way is right for you, begin the men's work that many of us, fathers, brothers, husbands and sons, have put off for too long. Together, we can become the radical love and compassion that mental health counselor Jay Sefton speaks of.

All we have to do is *open the door.*

# *RESOURCES*

**National Sexual Assault Services Hotline**
**Rape, Abuse & Incest National Network (RAINN)**
www.rainn.org - 800.656.HOPE (4673)

**Gender equality**
**Promundo - promundoglobal.org**
**A Call to Men - www.acalltomen.org**
**Better Man Conference - bettermanconference.com**
**Catalyst - Catalyst.org**

**For men seeking a men's group:**
**The ManKind Project - mankindproject.org**
**Evryman - evryman.com**
**Humen - wearehumen.org**

**On relational practices:**
**The Taos Institute - www.TaosInstitute.net**

**Books**
*Deep Secrets* by Niobe Way
*When Boys Become Boys* by Judy Chu
*Men's Work: How to Stop the Violence That Tears Our Lives Apart* by Paul Kivel
*The Chalice and the Blade* by Riane Eisler

## MARK GREENE

Mark Greene has spent over a decade deconstructing our binary-riddled dialogues around manhood and masculinity. Mark consults to help men, individually and in organizations, create a healthier more connecting vision of masculine culture and identity. Mark and his partner, Dr. Saliha Bava, consult to organizations globally on diversity, inclusion, and relational practices.

Mark is the author of *Remaking Manhood* and *The Little #MeToo Book for Men*. Mark is co-author with his partner Dr. Saliha Bava, of *The Relational Book for Parenting*.

Mark writes and speaks about men's issues at *The Good Men Project, Salon, Shriver Report, Uplift Connect, Medium, Yes! Magazine, BBC* and the *New York Times*.

For more information, go to RemakingManhood.com.

Follow Mark on most social media @RemakingManhood

**"...vivid storytelling..."**

"Mark interweaves his own deeply personal stories with a salient and powerful deconstruction of manhood in America."
—Lisa Hickey, CEO, Good Men Project

REMAKING MANHOOD

Stories From the Front Lines of Change

**Mark Greene**
Executive Editor
The Good Men Project

Available at amazon

## *ALSO FROM MARK GREENE*

**Remaking Manhood** is a collection of Good Men Project Senior Editor Mark Greene's most popular articles on parenting, fatherhood and manhood. *Also available at Barnes & Noble Online.*

> "This is writing that unites men rather than dividing or exploiting them. It speaks to the very best part of men and asks them to bring that part to the fore—as fathers, as sons, as brothers, as husbands, as friends, as lovers, and as citizens of life."
> **—Michael Rowe, author of Other Men's Sons**

Made in the USA
Columbia, SC
10 December 2022

72371562R00046